A Fly in the Sky

Dedication

To my fabulous family—thank you for giving me wings.

Published by DAWN Publications
14618 Tyler Foote Road
Nevada City, CA 95959
916 292-3482

Library of Congress Cataloging-in-Publication
(Prepared by Quality Books, Inc.)

Pratt, Kristin Joy.
    A fly in the sky / Kristin Joy Pratt.
    p. cm.
    SUMMARY: A joyful exploration of birds, insects, and other
    animals of the air.
    ISBN: 1-883220-39-4 (pbk.)
    ISBN: 1-883220-40-8 (hard)

1. Animals—Juvenile literature. 2. Animal flight—Juvenile
literature. I. Title.

QL49.P73 1996   591
                                         QBI95-20600

Printed on recycled paper using soy based ink

Printed in Hong Kong

10 9 8 7 6 5 4 3 2 1
First Edition

Designed by LeeAnn Brook
Type style is Berkeley

Introduction

The air we breathe is a silent, invisible ocean flowing around us. How often do we notice it? Perhaps we become momentarily aware of its gentleness as we watch children fly kites in a park, or remember its awesome power in the midst of a blustery storm. Yet do we consider the air to be part of a global atmosphere?

Pure, dry air is made up of a few basic elements. It contains roughly 78 percent nitrogen, 21 percent oxygen, and one percent other gases. It also contains water vapor. These days, however, all air is not so pure, which makes it increasingly important to view the earth's air as one fragile unit.

Large-scale industrial air pollution causes the air in some areas to be nearly unbreathable. The most conspicuous form of air pollution is known as low-altitude ozone. The natural location of ozone is high in the upper atmosphere, where it protects terrestrial life from the sun's harmful ultraviolet rays. In the last few decades, man has discovered that this gas is created at low altitudes as well. Hydrocarbons from vehicle exhausts combine with nitrogen oxides and sunlight to produce damaging levels of ozone in the toxic murky haze known to most of us as smog. Not long ago, there was so much of it in Mexico City that birds fell dead in an inner-city park. City authorities were forced to declare a state of emergency and close schools.

What can be done to clean up our air? Is this global dilemma out of the reach of young people? Must we remain victims until we come of age? I do not believe so. Mankind's greatest weapon against mindless degradation is planted deeply within every one of us. It is the power of thought. We all possess the potential to think purely, perceptively, and powerfully. Within even the smallest thought lies the beginning of action.

We cannot continue to suppose thought, action, and atmosphere to be unrelated, when in reality they are closely linked. Because we are all part of the problem, we are necessarily all part of the solution. It is up to all of us to translate clear thinking into clear, decisive action, which must result in clear air.

Kristin Joy Pratt
1996

*I*f **Daphne the Damselfly**
flew into the sky,
And if she flew low
and if she flew high,
What do you think
that Daphne would spy?

Damselflies are similar to dragonflies, though much smaller
and thinner. Both have large compound eyes, so they see
extremely well. They have six legs, four wings, and a long, thin
abdomen. Damselflies and dragonflies have lived on Earth for
200 million years, and have not changed much in that time.
They still must hold their wings out from their bodies, while
other more advanced insects such as katydids and ladybugs
can fold their wings onto their backs to protect them from
damage. Yet dragonflies and damselflies can move each wing
independently, which allows them to fly both forward and
backward like a hummingbird, as well as hover in mid
air. Both inhabit lakes, ponds, swamps and rivers
all over the world.

A

She'd admire an awesome airborne **Albatross,**

The Wandering Albatross is an impressive expression of grace. Its wingspan, which extends up to eleven feet, is the widest of any animal living on the planet. True to its name, the Wandering Albatross spends most of its life in flight. It soars on wind currents over vast distances of ocean, covering up to three hundred miles in one day. This gargantuan glider lands on the ocean only in calm weather, feasting on fish, squid, and the food refuse from ships. The drifting path of the Albatross leads it to land only to nest and to bring up its young. This is done in the sublime seclusion of several subantarctic isles. Because it takes eleven weeks for the chicks to incubate, breeding is only possible every other year. However, the average life span of the Wandering Albatross is more than thirty years.

And behold a bragging **Blue-Footed Booby** boasting his beautiful feet.

B

The Blue-Footed Booby's curious name comes from an English version of the Spanish word for clown, which is *bobo*. To impress their partners, as this booby seems to be doing, they strut around, showing off their brilliant blue feet. Boobies are large seabirds specifically adapted for dramatic plunge-diving. The tapered body, long wings and tail, and sleek, pointed bill enable boobies to fish underwater. Blue-footed Boobies live among some of the smaller Galapagos Islands, in the remote Pacific 600 miles from South America. They nest in small colonies and lay two to three eggs at a time. They feed close to shore, unlike other boobies. Baby boobies eat partially digested fish regurgitated by their parents.

She could creep up on a couple of cavorting courting **Cranes**,

C

All cranes are spectacular dancers. The Sandhill Crane is a particularly elegant and graceful bird. This four foot crane bows, hops, and leaps as much as 15 to 20 feet into the air in the course of its performance. Pairs dance together during mating season, but at other times, hundreds of birds may join together in spontaneous collective performances. In the summer, Sandhill Cranes reside in northeast Siberia, Canada, Alaska, and other northern parts of the United States. They move as far south as central Mexico during cold weather. The actual color of the Sandhill Crane is gray and white, although the adults in some areas have turned rusty brown due to a peculiar feeding habit. They probe with their bills into mud and soil containing rust-colored iron oxide. When they preen, the cranes spread the staining mineral all over their bodies.

Or discover a dynamic **Flying Dragon.**

Several types of animals which are not birds also fly, glide and swoop through the air. The Flying Dragon is a lizard which frequently glides from branch to branch. It inhabits many of the lush forests of Southeast Asia and uses the brightly colored flaps of skin on the sides of its body as a sort of built-in parachute. Its tail acts like a rudder, helping the lizard to steer while gliding. The Flying Dragon's vision is very advanced, which enables it to locate and catch insects in the dim light of the dense forest. Unlike most other gliders, such as flying possums and frogs, the Flying Dragon sleeps in the night and is active during the day.

D

E

She'd even encounter two excited emblematic Eagles,

In 1782, the American Bald Eagle was declared the national emblem of the United States. Nevertheless, the Bald Eagle has often not been treated by Americans with respect. Eagle populations decreased until President Kennedy appealed to the people in 1963 to save the Bald Eagle from destruction. "The fierce beauty and proud independence of this great bird aptly symbolize the strength and freedom of America," he said, "and we shall have failed a trust if we allow the eagle to disappear." At that time, many Bald Eagles had also fallen victim to toxic chemicals such as DDT. There were fewer than 400 nesting pairs left in the continental United States. Today the Bald Eagle's future looks considerably brighter. Thanks to years of protection, more than 4,000 nesting pairs now survive in the continental United States, with upwards of 45,000 more Bald Eagles in Alaska.

And find five fuzzy feasting
Fruit Bats munching on mangoes.

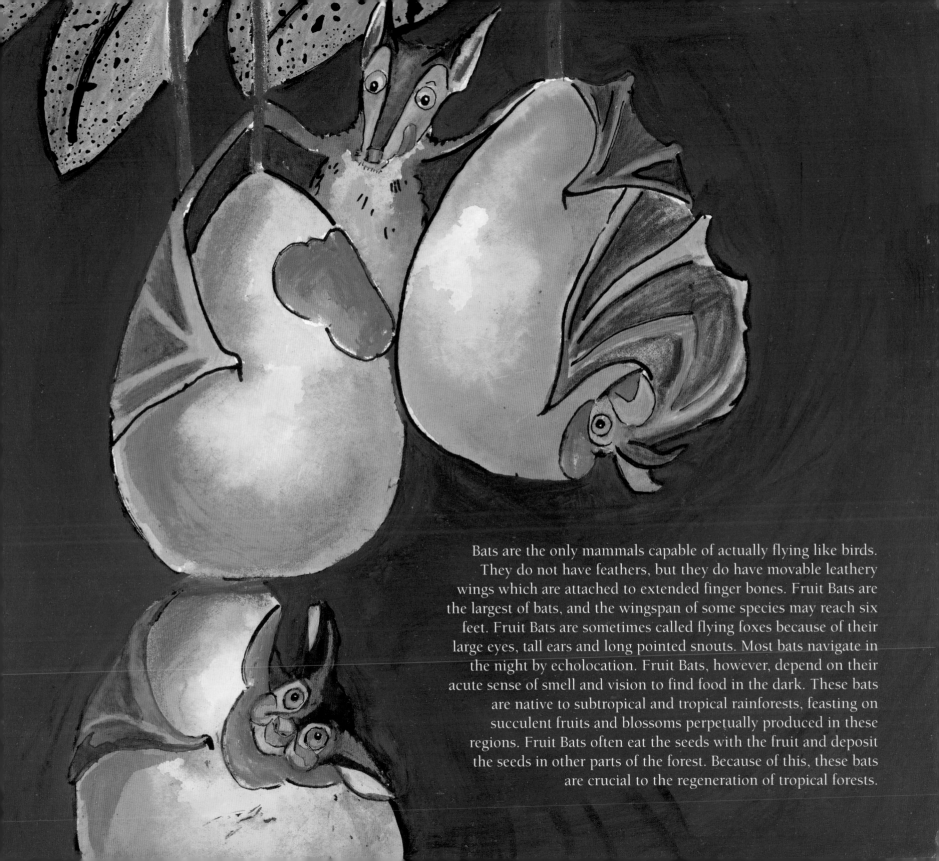

Bats are the only mammals capable of actually flying like birds. They do not have feathers, but they do have movable leathery wings which are attached to extended finger bones. Fruit Bats are the largest of bats, and the wingspan of some species may reach six feet. Fruit Bats are sometimes called flying foxes because of their large eyes, tall ears and long pointed snouts. Most bats navigate in the night by echolocation. Fruit Bats, however, depend on their acute sense of smell and vision to find food in the dark. These bats are native to subtropical and tropical rainforests, feasting on succulent fruits and blossoms perpetually produced in these regions. Fruit Bats often eat the seeds with the fruit and deposit the seeds in other parts of the forest. Because of this, these bats are crucial to the regeneration of tropical forests.

G

She'd glide by a gargantuan gangling **Gallinule**

The Purple Gallinule is a chicken-sized swamp bird. It nests in reeds along the edge of swamps and lakes in southern Spain, Portugal, and the island of Sardinia in the Mediterranean. Its ducklike bill helps it to uproot tasty tender shoots of swamp plants, while the gallinule's gargantuan feet allow it to wade in deep water and hop over slippery lily pads. The gallinule walks much like a heron due to its lanky legs. It raises each foot all the way out of the knee-deep water before placing it down again. This careful motion makes it appear as if the bird is perpetually stalking something. The Purple Gallinule emits weird shrieking and hooting sounds as well.

And hide from a hungry hunting **Heron**.

The Green-backed Heron is usually a secretive species, slinking among dense marsh vegetation and feeding mainly at night. It uses its powerful, stabbing bill to catch frogs and small fish. It lives worldwide in tropical and subtropical regions. During mating season, Green-backed Herons congregate in small loose groups to build their nests in low trees or bushes overhanging water. They are clumsy nest builders; one might get as good a look at the two to four eggs from beneath the loose pile of twigs as from above it.

H

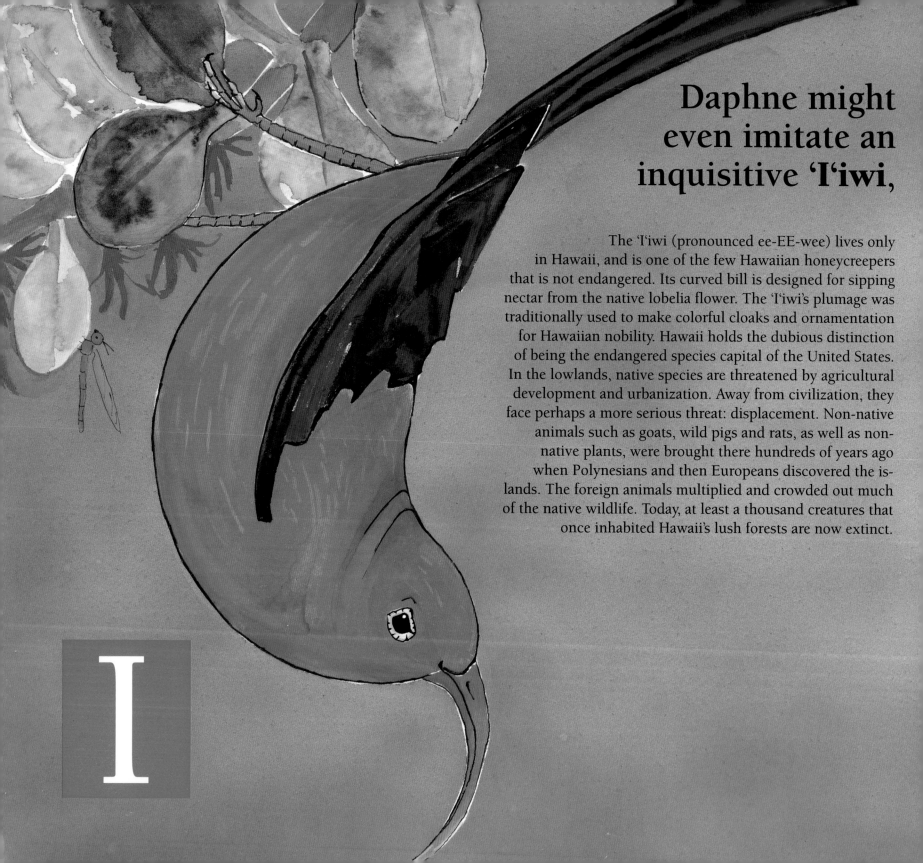

Daphne might even imitate an inquisitive 'I'iwi,

The 'I'iwi (pronounced ee-EE-wee) lives only in Hawaii, and is one of the few Hawaiian honeycreepers that is not endangered. Its curved bill is designed for sipping nectar from the native lobelia flower. The 'I'iwi's plumage was traditionally used to make colorful cloaks and ornamentation for Hawaiian nobility. Hawaii holds the dubious distinction of being the endangered species capital of the United States. In the lowlands, native species are threatened by agricultural development and urbanization. Away from civilization, they face perhaps a more serious threat: displacement. Non-native animals such as goats, wild pigs and rats, as well as non-native plants, were brought there hundreds of years ago when Polynesians and then Europeans discovered the islands. The foreign animals multiplied and crowded out much of the native wildlife. Today, at least a thousand creatures that once inhabited Hawaii's lush forests are now extinct.

I

Or joke with a jovial **Junco**.

All five forms of the pert little Dark-eyed Junco sing musical trills, and twitter rapidly in flight. The colorings of these different subspecies vary dramatically, yet all possess white bellies, white outer tail feathers, and, as their name suggests, profoundly dark eyes. The Dark-eyed Junco breeds in Canada, as well as in the north and central portions of the United States. In the winter, it journeys as far south as Mexico. It feasts primarily on seeds, but may obtain additional protein by eating plump, tasty insects during nesting season.

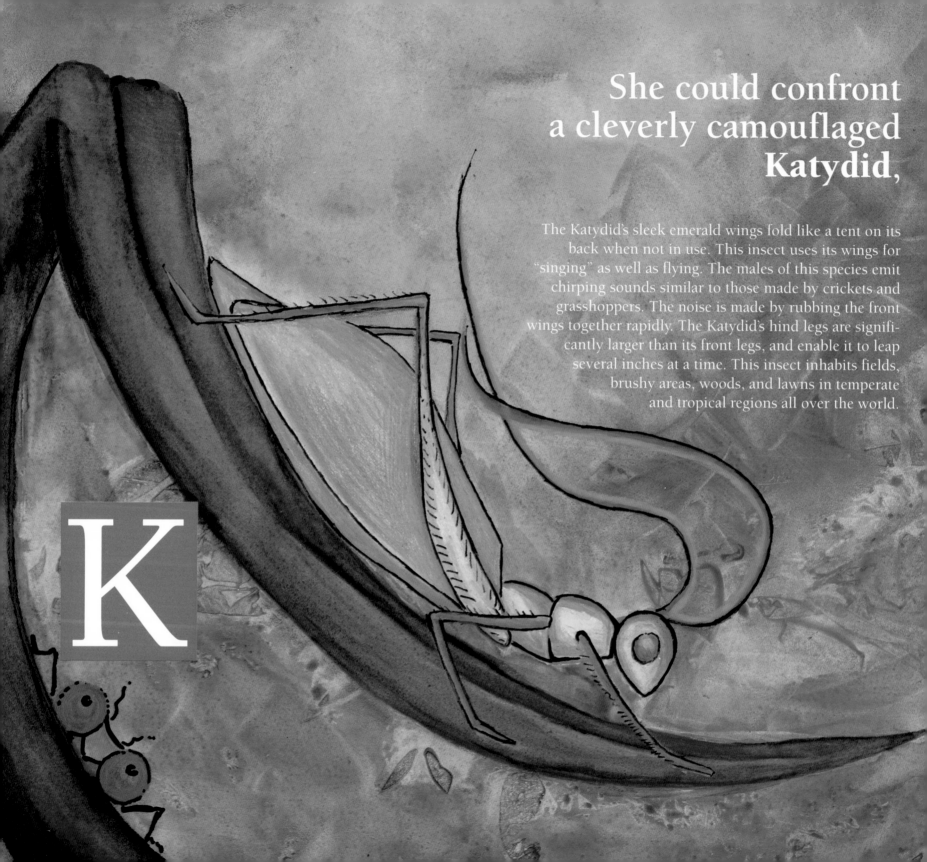

She could confront a cleverly camouflaged **Katydid,**

The Katydid's sleek emerald wings fold like a tent on its back when not in use. This insect uses its wings for "singing" as well as flying. The males of this species emit chirping sounds similar to those made by crickets and grasshoppers. The noise is made by rubbing the front wings together rapidly. The Katydid's hind legs are significantly larger than its front legs, and enable it to leap several inches at a time. This insect inhabits fields, brushy areas, woods, and lawns in temperate and tropical regions all over the world.

K

L

And linger along a line of little **Ladybugs**.

The ladybug is a favorite insect ally of gardeners in temperate regions all over the world because it controls pests without the use of pesticides. Ladybugs eat soft-bodied aphids in vast quantities. As they grow up, the baby ladybugs develop from spiny juveniles into sleek, red adults with characteristic black spots. The ladybug has two pairs of wings. The outer pair are tough, rigid, and not used for flying. They act as a protective shell for the second pair of wings underneath.

She might meet a magnificently metallic **Morpho Butterfly.**

Morpho Butterflies are well known for their metallic blue wings. Only the males, however, possess this incredible coloring. The butterfly pictured here is a male *Morpho rhetenor*, one of five morpho species. It has a maximum wingspan of five and a half inches. Male Morphos are collected by the millions each year for use in jewelry. Adorned in more subdued earthtones, the females of each species have evolved their own unique coloring to help them camouflage with the surrounding foliage. *Rhetenor* females are orange, yellow, and brown. They lay their eggs on grasses such as bamboo in the rainforests of Central and South America.

N

She'd notice a nifty nocturnal **Nectar Bat,**

At two and a half inches long, the Long-tongued Nectar Bat is one of the smallest plant-eating bats. It has a long tongue and a thin, pointed nose which help it to carefully slurp the sweet nectar out of blossoms such as the red-orange bottle brush. The Nectar Bat is a vital pollinator in its habitat: rainforests of Thailand, the Solomon Islands, and northern Australia. It roosts in the leaves of banana trees and hemp plants. In some areas, the Long-tongued Nectar Bat can bear young during any season.

And observe an ochre-eyed **Owl.**

Clad in striking white, the Snowy Owl is perfectly cam-
ouflaged for its environment. This owl with catlike eyes
inhabits the freezing tundra zone surrounding the North
Pole. The fluctuating population cycles of the local
lemmings (brown fuzzy rodents which constitute the
main staple of the bird's diet) govern the Snowy Owl's
breeding performances, population, and distribu-
tion. Most hunting is done at dawn and dusk.
The female Snowy Owl, as pictured here, is
larger and displays more decorated
plumage than males, which are as
much as twenty percent smaller
and totally white.

P

Daphne would perceive a profusion of plummeting **Pelicans**,

Brown Pelicans plummet into the warm waters of the Caribbean Sea in search of food. Unlike any other pelican, the Brown Pelican dives anywhere from ten to thirty-three feet into the ocean. Its expandable throat pouch allows it to get a whole fish in its mouth at once. Brown Pelicans nest in great colonies on the ground, on coastal cliffs, or even in trees. During the mating ceremony, males collect nesting materials to present ritually to their partners. The female then lays two to three white eggs, which hatch after a month of incubation. The young fly from the nest eleven to twelve weeks later. Brown Pelicans inhabit both the Pacific and Atlantic coasts of North and South America, and can also be found on the Galapagos Islands as well as on several Caribbean isles.

Or discover a quaintly curious **Quail**.

The male Montezuma Quail is handsomely adorned with stripes and spots, and sports a flaming yellow crest. The female's plumage is a more subtle blend of warm grays and dusty peach. They inhabit the mountainous arid regions of the American Southwest. Montezuma Quails are very well adapted to the persistent lack of moisture, and can do without water for long periods. They have stocky feet, which they use for digging up juicy tubers and roots which serve as vital sources of liquid. This adaptation is the key to survival in the harsh desert environment. The birds call to each other with gentle whistles.

Q

She'd regard a red **Rosella**,

The brilliantly colored Crimson Rosella inhabits eucalyptus forests of eastern Australia. Both the female and the male are adorned with intense crimson plumage, as their name suggests, and with deep indigo and royal blue accents. The young flash bright yellow-green until they grow their adult plumage. Adolescent Rosellas lead a nomadic lifestyle in groups of up to thirty. The more mature generations settle down and usually reside in small, permanent colonies.

R

Spy a shiny sunning
Swallowtail,

S

Unlike other insect species, butterflies can
see a full range of color. This helps them
locate favorite flowers. Some may prefer certain
colored flowers over others. The Swallowtail group contains several different
species, including the largest butterfly
in the world, Queen Alexandra's
Birdwing. It measures eleven
inches across. The butterfly
pictured here is the more common Tiger Swallowtail, which
inhabits deserts, grasslands, forests,
and gardens alike. Swallowtails are a
unique group of butterflies, and their
welfare is considered a reflection of the
quality of their environment. These
butterflies reflect ecological trends in
tropical rainforests. The Queen Alexandra's
Birdwing is now classified as an endangered
species. The biggest threat to Swallowtails is
deforestation, with commercial collection
and poaching not far behind.

And tarry with a terrific Gliding Tree Frog.

Tree frogs are famous for their extraordinary leaps. Gliding Tree Frogs can jump farther than any other tree frog, an ability which helps them to escape predators. They have special webs between their toes which allow them to glide long distances. When the frogs spread out their toes, each foot acts like a tiny blue and black spotted kite. In this manner, Gliding Tree Frogs can glide from tree to tree, or from a high perch to the ground. Several small suction cups on the sole of each foot ensure solid landings for the little leapers.

U

She'd greet an utterly unflappable Ultramarine Grosbeak,

The male Ultramarine Grosbeak, as pictured here, is a striking shade of blue, and the female is a warm cocoa brown with lighter underparts. Ultramarines are very similar to Blue-black Grosbeaks, though much smaller. They usually live together in pairs, and occasionally perch prominently on top of bushes or trees in the early morning hours. Males have a fairly loud musical song which is slow at first, then slurs characteristically downward. Though fairly common in the undergrowth and woodland edges of eastern South America, the Ultramarine Grosbeak is reclusive and very hard to spot.

View a very vain **Vulture**,

The King Vulture's striking black and white plumage, combined with the strangely beautiful pigments of its head and neck, easily qualify this scavenger of tropical forests as one of the most colorful of all the birds of prey. It locates animal remains chiefly by virtue of its excellent sense of smell. Though fairly common from central Mexico to northern Argentina, the King Vulture is often difficult to spot because of its solitary nature and high flight altitude. The King Vulture is only slightly smaller than the stately Bald Eagle.

V

W

And watch a wonderful winging **Whydah**.

During mating season, the six inch male Paradise Whydah of central Africa grows an extraordinary display of ink black tail feathers which measure almost twice as long as its body. He uses his impressive tail, combined with the dynamic coloration of his chest and throat, to perform an exquisite courtship performance for the sparrowlike female. He circles above her head, waving his tail plumes up and down in undulating flight. The female lays her eggs in the nests of unsuspecting Green-winged Pytilias, which raise the young whydahs with their own chicks.

X

She'd examine an extraordinary Xantus' Hummingbird

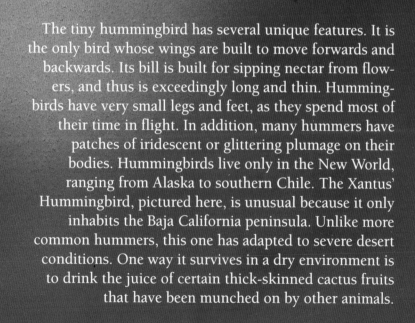

The tiny hummingbird has several unique features. It is the only bird whose wings are built to move forwards and backwards. Its bill is built for sipping nectar from flowers, and thus is exceedingly long and thin. Hummingbirds have very small legs and feet, as they spend most of their time in flight. In addition, many hummers have patches of iridescent or glittering plumage on their bodies. Hummingbirds live only in the New World, ranging from Alaska to southern Chile. The Xantus' Hummingbird, pictured here, is unusual because it only inhabits the Baja California peninsula. Unlike more common hummers, this one has adapted to severe desert conditions. One way it survives in a dry environment is to drink the juice of certain thick-skinned cactus fruits that have been munched on by other animals.

Y

Yield to a yapping
Yellow-Bellied Glider,

There are six species of gliding possums which inhabit
eucalyptus forests of New Guinea
and Australia. These soaring marsupi-
als make their homes in the cavities of
enormous elderly eucalypti. It takes 120
years for eucalyptus trees to develop hollow
cavities in which the gliders can nest. Yellow-
bellied Gliders can cover over 100 yards in one
swoop, with the help of furry skin that stretches
between their fore and hind legs. They pair for life,
marking each other with scent glands on their
foreheads, chests, and rears. Although adults weigh
only a few ounces, each family requires around 100
acres of forage space, and will not tolerate intruders
from other groups. Yet the Yellow-bellied Glider is
very friendly with other members of its family.

And slip into the zone of a zany **Zebra Butterfly** zealously zipping on a flower!

The Zebra Longwing is a very distinctive butterfly. The bold coloration and unique flight pattern of this insect set it apart from any other butterfly. Its long, narrow wings are banded with intense yellow stripes, and speckled around the edges with colorful spots. The Zebra Longwing's usual flight is slow and wafting, with extremely shallow wingbeats. When alarmed, however, it can make good speed as it dodges expertly to cover. Zebra Longwings roost in colonies at night, assembling during dusk. During the day, they scatter again to feed. This butterfly feeds on passion flowers, and hatches multiple broods throughout the year. The range of the Zebra Longwing includes southern portions of North America, as well as most of tropical America.

Z

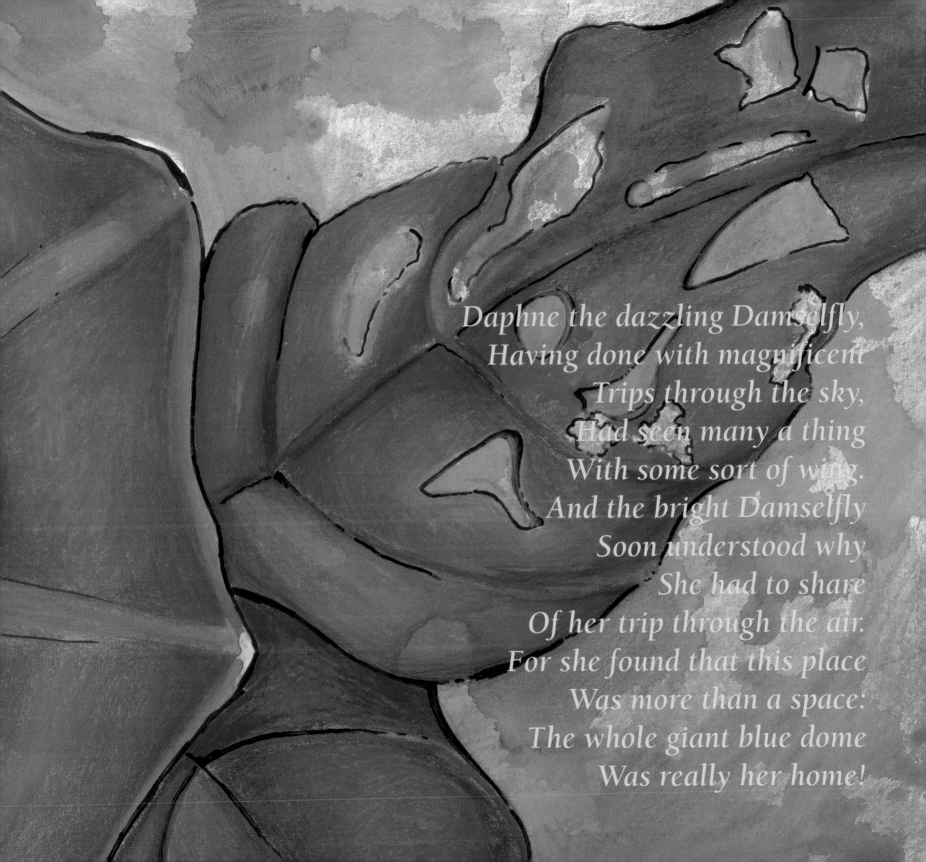

Daphne the dazzling Damselfly,
Having done with magnificent
Trips through the sky,
Had seen many a thing
With some sort of wing.
And the bright Damselfly
Soon understood why
She had to share
Of her trip through the air.
For she found that this place
Was more than a space:
The whole giant blue dome
Was really her home!

About the Author

A published book is the dream of every aspiring author. Producing three books before you graduate from college is a truly extraordinary accomplishment. For 19-year-old Kristin Joy Pratt this achievement is the outcome of her belief that anything is possible if you devote sufficient time and energy, and refuse to be distracted by limiting thoughts.

A Walk in the Rainforest, published when Kristin was 15 years old, was called "a stunning alphabet book" by **Parents Magazine.** After **A Swim Through the Sea** was released when Kristin was 17 years old, **E Magazine** inducted her into The Kid Heroes Hall of Fame. Since then Kristin has maintained a full college schedule of classes and activities while writing and illustrating **A Fly in the Sky**. In her "spare" time Kristin has continued to tour, appearing as a keynote speaker at a variety of conferences and schools. She especially enjoys bringing her message of environmental concern to large numbers of school children. Both through her books and in her personal life, Kristin is an outstanding role model for today's young people.

Acknowledgments

I would like to express my heartfelt gratitude for the many friends and family members who have helped make this work possible—especially Rachel Crandell, Glenn Felch, Kathy Pratt, Katie Pratt, Ken Pratt, Kevin Pratt, the helpful St. Louis Zoo Library staff, and my great friends at DAWN Publications for their extraordinary patience and guidance.

DAWN Publications is dedicated to helping people experience a sense of unity and harmony with all life. Each of our products encourages a deeper sensitivity and appreciation for the natural world. For a copy of our free catalog listing all of our products, please call 800-545-7475.